Nat's Inspirational Treats

Nat's Inspirational Treats

Words of Encouragement for Kids in Business

NATALEE S. WILLIAMS

*"You're never too young
to expand your ideas."*

– Natalee Williams

COPYRIGHT 2013—NATALEE S. WILLIAMS

Printed and bound in the United States of America.

All rights reserved. No part of this book may be reproduced or transmitted in any form or by any means, electronic or mechanical, including photocopying, recording or by any information storage and retrieval system,(except by a reviewer who may quote brief passages in a review to be printed in a magazine, newspaper, or on the web) without written permission from the publisher.

ISBN-10: 0-9978541-8-9
ISBN-13: 978-0-9978541-8-3

Unless otherwise indicated, all Scripture quotations are taken from the King James Version of the Bible.

For additional information contact:
Nat's Sweet Treats via email: natsweettreats@yahoo.com

Book Copyedited, Coordinated and Published by:
Theresa Royal Brown
Royal Brown Publishing

Cover Photo Credit:
Maynard Manzano
Magic Glamour Photography

SPECIAL NOTE: To all churches, schools and professional organizations: Quantity discounts are available on bulk purchases of this book for educational or gift purposes.

To my parents, family, friends
and all kids in business.
I hope my book inspires you.

Table of Contents

Introduction.........................1

Chapter One: Struggles and Sacrifices......3

Chapter Two: Hope and Faith............7

Chapter Three: Work Hard And Play Hard...11

Chapter Four: Staying Focused...........15

Chapter Five: Believe In Yourself.........19

Chapter Six: The Golden Rule...........23

Chapter Seven: Be You – An Original.....27

Chapter Eight: Words Can Hurt.........31

Table of Contents (Continued)

Chapter Nine: Stay Humble 35

Chapter Ten: Be Careful and Prayerful 39

Chapter Eleven: Follow God's Way 43

Final Inspirational Treat 47

Acknowledgments: 49

About The Author 51

Introduction

As a young entrepreneur, have you ever needed words of encouragement during a rough time in your life? Have you ever felt like no one knew or understood what challenges you face as a young person in business? Have you ever woken up in the morning thinking it was going to be a bad day, but you see the sunshine and suddenly you felt great?

We've all needed the sun to shine in our lives, especially when it seemed as though there was darkness all around. That ray of sun was our encouragement, and this book is also a source of inspiration as well.

Young entrepreneurs in business need words to uplift their spirits and help them when times are hard.

That is what this book is for, to encourage you to be confident in yourself and go after your dreams in spite of any obstacles, circumstances or tough decisions you must face.

If you ever run into a difficult situation and you need encouragement, this book is the perfect tool to get you back on track.

Chapter One
Struggles and Sacrifices

Young entrepreneurs face many struggles and sacrifices. Some struggles are balancing school work, church, after school activities and running your own business.

School work should be your main priority because without a proper education, you can't grow and advance to the next level in your life and/or business.

Ask yourself the question: "What is the best way to balance school work and business."

1. Have a "To Do" List
2. Make a schedule
3. Have a calendar/agenda with you at all times

What are the sacrifices that need to be made when you are a young entrepreneur?

1. Less TV time
2. No staying up late doing unnecessary things
3. Reduced time on the phone talking to friends
4. Not a lot of time "hanging out" with friends
5. Little time to do after school activities

Even though you will have struggles and sacrifices, always remember that your hard work will pay off.

Inspirational Treat:

"I can do all things through Christ who strengthens me." Philippians 4:13

Take a Closer Look at Yourself

What did you learn from this chapter and what are you inspired to do next?

_____

_____

_____

_____

_____

_____

_____

_____

Chapter Two
Hope and Faith

You must have hope as well as faith in order to succeed in life and business.

This means to move forward toward your destiny and keep pushing until you make your mark. It is important to encourage others by the example that you set.

By praying, reading God's word, speaking declarations over your life and showing God's love, you are showing others that you indeed have hope and faith.

Inspirational Treat:

"Now faith is the substance of things hoped for, the evidence of things not seen." Hebrews 11:1

Take a Closer Look at Yourself

What did you learn from this chapter and what are you inspired to do next?

_____

_____

_____

_____

_____

_____

_____

_____

Chapter Three
Work Hard And Play Hard

In life, you must work hard and play hard.

As young entrepreneurs, this statement of working hard to play hard is not something that everyone wants to do. It is also very hard to do because playing with friends and having fun are the things most children want to do. Working on business plans, products, "to do" lists and schedules are not things that are fun and no one wants to do it.

However, being in business for yourself requires that you sometimes do things that you really don't want to do in order to get things that others don't have.

Hard work is necessary but playing hard and getting time to enjoy the things you are able to get from your hard work, keeps you balanced and reduces stress.

Always Work Hard and Play Just As Hard!!!

Inspirational Treat:

"Lazy hands make a man poor, diligent hands bring wealth." Proverbs 10:4

Take a Closer Look at Yourself

What did you learn from this chapter and what are you inspired to do next?

_____

_____

_____

_____

_____

_____

_____

_____

Chapter Four
Staying Focused

Focus! Get things done!

It is important to stay focused on the task you must complete especially as a young entrepreneur.

As a young person, you have so many distractions that can get you off track.

STAY FOCUSED!

How can I stay focused?

1. Turn off the TV and phone
2. No video or computer games
3. Stop daydreaming
4. Don't procrastinate

Staying focused is your guaranteed way to success!

Inspirational Treat:

"I press towards the mark for the prize of the high calling of God in Christ Jesus." Philippians 3:14

Take a Closer Look at Yourself

What did you learn from this chapter and what are you inspired to do next?

_____

_____

_____

_____

_____

_____

_____

_____

Chapter Five
Believe In Yourself

Really think about these words: "Be confident and believe in yourself." When you show that you are confident in what you are doing, others will believe in it as well and will support you. Always show confidence when you meet new people or speak about your business to others. Remember, confidence is the key to your success.

It is important to remember the following:

- Never be afraid of your opinion.
- Always stand up for yourself.

- Show others what you're made of.
- Don't say negative things about yourself.

Never give up on yourself, that's the most important thing to remember, never give up! God has so many things in store for you! He loves you, he will help you, he will bless you, he will do the impossible, he cares for you, he will give you strength, he will give you joy, he will give you grace, and peace.

You are special and you should believe that you are. Believe in yourself and never give up on God!

Inspirational Treat:

"Don't let anyone look down on you because you are young, but set an example for the believers...."
1 Timothy 4:12-14

Take a Closer Look at Yourself

What did you learn from this chapter and what are you inspired to do next?

_____

_____

_____

_____

_____

_____

_____

_____

Chapter Six
The Golden Rule

Treat others the way you want to be treated because it is the golden rule. However, not everyone shows respect to others, especially when it is someone you don't like. You must show respect even when someone is not being nice to you.

Often people are rude because someone has been rude to them first. Show kindness at all times and be the change you want to see in others.

It is also important to show respect to others because in the bible, God says "Love one another with brotherly affection. Outdo one another in showing honor." Romans 12:10

You can show respect by not spreading rumors, not gossiping, not cyberbullying or bullying others at school. Show respect to others everywhere and at all times, show people that you care about them and that you follow the golden rule.

Inspirational Treat:

"*But I say to you, love your enemies and pray for those who persecute you.*" Matthew 5:44

Take a Closer Look at Yourself

What did you learn from this chapter and what are you inspired to do next?

_____

_____

_____

_____

_____

_____

_____

_____

_____

Chapter Seven
Be You – An Original

Be who YOU are because that is the ONLY person you can be. Also, be an original, not a copy of someone else. Being you may not be easy, but guess what? Being yourself shows others that you love yourself for who you are, no matter what others think of you.

Sometimes, people dislike others because they're not honest about themselves. Being yourself shows others what you're capable of and you appreciate the gifts, talents, and blessings that you have. It is important to be yourself because you are special and no one will ever take that away from you. You are you!

Don't try to change for others or "fit in" with the crowd by lying about the things you really like to do that may seem boring or not cool to others. You must always be true to yourself so you won't be false to others.

BE TRUE AND BE YOU!

> *Inspirational Treat:*
>
> *"I praise you for I am fearfully and wonderfully made."* Psalms 139:14

Take a Closer Look at Yourself

What did you learn from this chapter and what are you inspired to do next?

_____

_____

_____

_____

_____

_____

_____

_____

Chapter Eight

Words Can Hurt

Have you ever heard of the phrase, *"Sticks and stones may break my bones but, words can never hurt me."* Unfortunately this statement is not true because words can hurt. Words are powerful because they can bring someone down or build someone up.

It is important to not hurt others with your words because words are powerful and they do influence people easily.

You should not talk about others, especially behind their back, because you just never know what they are going through or what is going on in their life. Also, you wouldn't want others talking about you, now would you?

How can your words hurt others? Spreading rumors, gossip, lies, and just saying negative things about someone can hurt people. Be very careful with what you say, because you just never know who you might hurt.

> ## Inspirational Treat:
> *"A gentle answer turns away wrath, but a harsh word stirs up anger."* Provers 15:1

Take a Closer Look at Yourself

What did you learn from this chapter and what are you inspired to do next?

_____

_____

_____

_____

_____

_____

_____

_____

Chapter Nine

Stay Humble

Some of you reading this book already have your own business. What you must remember is that you didn't start your business by yourself, and many people have helped you. Always remember to stay humble. Humble means to be modest and lower in pride. It means don't brag about yourself and what you have accomplished. Let others do it. In the bible, God says "Humble yourselves before the Lord and he will lift you up." James 4:10

Why is this so important, especially in business? It is important because just as God can bless you with your business or material things, He can easily take those things away.

Humility does not mean thinking less of yourself than of other people, nor does it mean having a low opinion of your own gifts. It means freedom from thinking about yourself at all. (William Temple) This statement is so very true and simply means don't be prideful, but appreciate the gifts that you have. Be confident in your abilities but always, always stay humble.

How can you stay humble? You can stay humble by appreciating your gifts, not bragging about yourself, by having reasonable confidence, even by praying about it and reading the bible.

Inspirational Treat:

"Humble yourselves before the Lord and he will lift you up." James 4:10

Take a Closer Look at Yourself

What did you learn from this chapter and what are you inspired to do next?

_____

_____

_____

_____

_____

_____

_____

_____

Chapter Ten

Be Careful and Prayerful

Be careful and prayerful in everything that you do so you won't get caught up in the wrong things in life.

These days there is a lot of peer pressure at school and things that we can easily get trapped into. Drugs, gangs, smoking, or hanging out with the wrong crowd are just a few things that can take us off track and make us miss out on achieving our goals. We constantly need to pray to ask God for direction.

Having your own business brings along its own set of responsibilities and other kids will look up to you and will follow what you do. This is where we must also be careful in the things we do, people we associate with and the decisions we make.

Praying is always the best decision because God will help you when you need him. Always know that you're not alone and God is always going to be there for you. Being careful and prayerful in all you do will pay off for you in the long run.

Inspirational Treat:

"Pray without ceasing." I Thessalonians 5:17

Take a Closer Look at Yourself

What did you learn from this chapter and what are you inspired to do next?

_____

_____

_____

_____

_____

_____

_____

_____

Chapter Eleven
Follow God's Way

It is important to follow God's way in everything you do because if you put God first, great things will be given to you.

Live God's word and follow his commandments.

How can you really follow God's way? You can follow God's way in your life and in your business by doing the following:

- Talk to God daily
- Talk to your friends about Him

- Read your bible
- Do your homework neatly and on time
- Don't be disrespectful to your parents or teachers
- Be kind to those you are serving
- Help out in church
- Obeying your parents
- And much more!

When you follow God's way, this will show up in your life and in your business, everything will fall into place and work out for the best.

Inspirational Treat:

"But seek first his kingdom and his righteousness and all these things will be given to you as well."
Matthew 6:33

Take a Closer Look at Yourself

What did you learn from this chapter and what are you inspired to do next?

_____

_____

_____

_____

_____

_____

_____

_____

Final Inspirational Treat

Thank you for reading my book and I hope it inspired you to keep striving for your dreams.

Keep working hard, believe in yourself, and never stop dreaming.

Remember, you're never too young to expand your ideas.

Also, when you need words of encouragement or if you need to be inspired and motivated, feel free to refer to this book.

Natalee

Acknowledgments:

First giving honor to **God** for His love and kindness to me.

To my parents, **Gerald and Barbara Williams,** for all their support and love. (I love you mom and dad!)

To my **Aunt Beverly Sargent,** for giving me my first interview for my fundraiser when I was 7 years old.

To my business mentor, **Theresa Royal Brown,** thank you for helping me build and grow my business.

To my former pastor, **Rev. Dr. Kenneth Hill** and **First Lady Janice Hill,** I thank you. Pastor

Hill, when I came to you with my idea to raise money for Haiti, after their devastating earthquake, you did not turn me away. You encouraged me to first come up with a plan. This led to my business being born.

To my **family and friends,** thank you for supporting me every step of the way.

To my **church family,** thank you for your love and care for me and my family and for keeping me on track.

I appreciate every single thing you all have done, and I love each and every one of you!

About The Author
Natalee S. Williams

Natalee S. Williams, has always had a heart for benevolence. When she was 7 years old, she single-handedly raised $140 in change for the Youth World Evangelism Action (YWEA), an international youth-led fundraising campaign. These funds were used to build a school in Rwanda and Kenya. When she heard the news report about Haiti's slow recovery after its terrible earthquake, she decided to do something about it. After speaking to her parents and her pastor, she devised a plan and set a goal to raise $300 by selling cupcakes after church services. With much prayer, hard work, and enthusiasm, the goal was met and surpassed. After the fundraising endeavor, Natalee began to receive numerous orders. She continued to watch the Food Network's Cupcake Wars, one of her favorite shows, and decided she too could start her own business. In the summer of 2011, Nat's Sweet Treats was born.

www.ingramcontent.com/pod-product-compliance
Lightning Source LLC
LaVergne TN
LVHW051512070426
835507LV00022B/3069